Prese

Oc

Transformation
in Prayer

"99 Words to Live By"

A series of fine gift books that presents inspirational words by renowned authors and captivating thinkers. Thought-provoking proverbs from many peoples and traditions complete each volume's collection.

"99 Words to Live By" explores topics that have moved and will continue to move people's hearts. Perfect for daily reflection as well as moments of relaxation.

Transformation
in Prayer

99 Sayings
by M. Basil Pennington

edited by

Jean Maalouf

New City Press
Hyde Park, New York

Published in the United States by New City Press
202 Cardinal Rd., Hyde Park, NY 12538
©2009 New City Press

Cover design by Leandro De Leon

Library of Congress Cataloging-in-Publication Data:

Pennington, M. Basil.
  Transformation in prayer : 99 sayings by   M. Basil
Pennington / edited by Jean Maalouf.
        p. cm.
  Includes bibliographical references and index.
  ISBN 978-1-56548-308-8 (pbk. : alk paper)   1. Prayer—
Christianity.   2. Pennington, M. Basil—Quotations.
I. Maalouf, Jean.   II. Title.
  BV210.3.P45 2008
  248.3'2—dc22   2008034432

Printed in Canada

M. Basil Pennington, O.C.S.O. (1931–2005), was a monk at St. Joseph's Abbey in Spencer, Massachusetts. He was a leading spiritual writer known especially for his work on centering prayer and on *lectio divina,* the ancient practice of praying the Scriptures. He was also recognized for his broad and dedicated religious search that led him to cross lines that divide denominations and different spiritual traditions. Indeed, he counted among his many friends rabbis from New York, Eastern Orthodox monks from Mount Athos, and Hindu spiritual masters from India. With all of them, Christians as well as those who profess other faiths, he sought to establish a frank dialogue that recognizes and respects the value of monasticism. And while he was concerned with finding ways to combine Eastern and Western spiritualities, his faith and devotion always remained Christocentric and Marian in character and aim.

In his ministry, Fr. Pennington used every medium available to communicate the good news of the gospel. He wrote sixty books and hundreds of articles, recorded videos and cassettes, preached retreats, gave interviews, and held audiences around the world. He also helped to begin projects such as translating the Cistercian Fathers into English, other studies in the area of Cistercian life and spirituality, as well as the "Cistercian Publications."

In the following pages, Fr. Pennington invites us, in a deeply personal way, to go deeper and deeper toward the Center where the Word of God speaks to us, where we experience God's healing love, and where real prayer takes place. Thence transformation is bound to occur, and a different world will emerge, reflecting a true self that sees things as God sees them. Here and now, we need such a selection of insights about our deepest longing — especially in a time of so much loneliness, stress, and violence, filled with so many deceptive mirages, never-satisfying achievements, and heartbreaking disappointments. It is refreshing to realize that, beyond the so-called "values" within which our world is enslaving us, there is true meaning to our lives so fulfilling, ecstatic, and liberating.

Jean Maalouf

"Master, I will follow you wherever you go." This is the basic attitude for centering prayer. We are willing to let go of everything and simply be to Jesus, with Jesus, wherever he leads. This is very simple and very pure love.

In centering prayer we get in touch with God at the very center of our being, the ground of our being, as the source. We come to know our true self as that beautiful person who at each moment comes forth from his creative love.

We need to be free from ourselves, from our false selves, projections and images, so that we can be open to reality in ourselves and in others. Right living will necessarily follow from true love and deep prayer.

During centering prayer, on some days there will be consolations that will make us feel very much at home during the prayer — the fox in his hole. But most days, that will probably not be the case. There will be little to satisfy the feelings and emotions. We may want to speak of dryness.

When through the transformation of consciousness that centering prayer brings about, through the activity of the Holy Spirit in his gifts, God has indeed become the context of our thinking, then all our thoughts and images will be alive and life-giving.

It isn't what we do or what we have or what others think of us that makes us. We are. On the contrary, instead of our being created by our doings and havings, with God we are the creative source that does whatever we want ("I can do all things in him who strengthens me") and has whatever we want ("Ask and you shall receive").

As we pray the rosary more formally, we ponder the most intimate mysteries of our faith-life, with the Hail Mary as the quiet background. We ask Mary to lead us into that fullness of understanding that she ultimately found, through a lived participation, and into that full sharing of the fruit of these saving mysteries that is preeminently hers in her complete freedom from sin and her corporeal glorification in the palace of her Son.

To say to God, "Lord, Lord," and then not to do what he wants, is to say words we do not mean. Rather than prayer, a true communication with God, our words are a lie. And no one who does not abide in the truth can enter into the kingdom of heaven.

It is through centering prayer that we open the space for the Holy Spirit to begin to act in us through his gifts. We gain a new perception, one that enables us to see what is beneath the surface. We begin to perceive in each person that which is of God in them, his beautiful image. We see each one, no matter how foolishly he or she may have acted, as the child beloved of the Father for whom he sent his Son to die. Spontaneously there begins to come to our lips the prayer of our Master: "Father, forgive them. They do not know what they are doing." We wish them well and pray for them.

Even enemies? Those who have deeply hurt us or, worse, have hurt those whom we love? That is what Jesus calls us to here. And yes, as our godlike perception grows through centering prayer, we see what Jesus sees in us sinners, someone beautiful enough to die for.

How many loaves do you have? Really, the number is not important. He can do as much with one as with seven. We all have the gift of life, the power to love, to be there with him for others. Given that, there is nothing we can't do with him, in him, through him....

How many loaves and fish do you have?

Take time to count them, thank God for each one, turn them over to him and courageously step forward to use them with him for the benefit of us all.

True centering prayer cannot but bring us into the kingdom of heaven. We may not experience it in any sensible way. But in faith we know it is so. And we will see it in our lives, as we become more and more determined to do the will of the Father in heaven.

It is a journey. At any point we can sit by the side of the road and take our rest. We can say: it is enough for me, or: it is enough for now. The only one who limits the joy, the peace and the light we enjoy is ourselves. Not God. God is all gift. He created only to give — to share divine happiness, which is all light, life and love. Jesus is leading each one of us. Perhaps others have first brought us to him. But as he takes us by the hand, our own faith and desire open us to receiving the light he wants to give us.

Do we think we are more capable than our Lord himself? How many times in the course of his few years of ministry did he not send the crowd away and flee away to a solitary place, even when everyone was seeking, seeking him with their very legitimate and pressing needs. Even the Son of man needed his time with the Father to be refreshed and renewed for his ministry.

One of the surprises
of centering prayer is
that we discover that God
can manage the world
for twenty minutes
without us — and
not mess it up too much!

Certainly a wonderful model for centering prayer is the little child in his father's arms. A true father is always delighted to have his little one in his arms. He doesn't much care if the child is squirming about a bit, looking this way and that or pulling his beard or just resting there or sleeping peacefully. As long as his child is there in his arms, the father is content.

Lord, let me see *again*. The Lord has told us: Unless you become as a little child you will not enter in. How did we see as a child before life began to distort our vision — maybe very violently distort it through the horror of child abuse and a dysfunctional family? Then we were able to look at things with an unprejudiced openness, letting things be as they truly are, trusting in the essential goodness of people. We relied completely on the providence of God incarnated then so exclusively in our parents. We had imagination and vision and limitless hope, we were open to all possibilities.

I do not emphasize prayer here to downplay the importance of other activities and efforts for disarmament and the pursuit of universal peace in justice and love. God does work in and through the activities and efforts of men and women. But we cannot sustain such activities and efforts if we do not have hope. Prayer renews our faith and lets us powerfully experience that we do have cause for hope.

In centering prayer we go right to the center, where Jesus ever dwells as our most intimate lover. He is there for us. And the little method of centering prayer ... helps us to bypass all the crowding thoughts and images and come to rest right there in the center with Jesus, to be healed by him and made whole.

We need to work at keeping a certain objectivity in our moral decisions. We need to avoid being wholly subjective, especially in a time when we are increasingly aware that our actions are often prompted by many unconscious motivations. True freedom lies in the appropriate relationship to reality; i.e., a clear perception of what reality is, and the ability to make responsible judgments and decisions in the light of that perception.

Centering prayer creates in us good, rich soil. In the moments of centering we are wide open to receive all that the Word has to give us. We let go of everything else; we are a boundless listening for the Word. And this attitude which we inculcate into our lives by the regular practice of centering prayer does indeed spread out through the rest of our lives.

When we sit down regularly to our centering — and during that centering, every time we become aware of anything else, we faithfully return to the Lord, gently using our love word — we begin to be steadfast in our intent. And what begins by fidelity to the prayer and in the prayer spreads out to the rest of our lives. Our whole heart's desire is for the Lord. We are good soil that is constantly asking for the enrichment of his grace.

Epiphany — letting reality be it-self to us. Not figuring it out or thinking it through. Just letting it be present, manifesting what it is. What is, is God, revealing his caring love in all. Even when what has been, has been disfig-ured and desecrated by sinful us, still, if its reality is allowed to shine, then from beneath the disfigurement God appears — is present. To be to this, to let God be to us — this is communion, this is prayer. Nothing more needs to be thought, said, or done. The mutual gift is pure, complete, and unimpeded. This is love: the complete gift of self and openness to the gift of the other. Mutual Epiphany.

In centering prayer we listen and listen and we do understand, through the activity of the Holy Spirit in the gifts. We look and look, and in a new way we perceive ourselves — as we are seen in the eyes of God — God himself, and every other person. Indeed, the whole of creation is perceived in a new way, as shot through with divinity. Then, indeed, *blessed are our eyes*. For we have what every upright person longs to see. Our hearts do understand, we change our ways, and we are fully healed.

The spirit of watching can be carried on beyond the actual time of prayer. As we shower, shave, and dress we can continue to meditate on some Scripture text, repeat some simple prayer, or simply abide in the Presence, longing for an ever greater presence. A household agreement that allows this to be a time of quiet without chatter, or the blare of radio, stereo, or television would greatly facilitate this. The watch could formally be concluded with a bit of family prayer at the breakfast table. In my Uncle Clark's home we had a psalm with a moment's reflection and a spontaneous prayer before we dived into our breakfast.

Being united to God, entering more fully into the experience of that union through prayer, is supposed to do something to us. We are not always comfortable with that transforming power. We tend to cling to what we have experienced ourselves having and being. But if we want to get to our deepest self, we have to go to the place where it originates. If we want to experience our deeper self, we have to experience the place of our origin and that is something ever new. For God ever calls us forth from nothingness.

As we sit in centering prayer, things do become clearer. It is not so much that we have brilliant insights; indeed, during the time of prayer we let all these things go. But there grows in us a deep sense that life does make sense. There is a certain unfolding. What has been hidden from us, the missing pieces of the puzzle of life, seem to show up. It is leavened all through. Something of the completeness, the allness, the peace of heaven begins to be present. God is at the center of our being. We let him truly be the Lord and Master of our domain. The kingdom of God is established within.

Things don't just happen. Ultimately, God is in charge. He has everything under control. How ontologically this all works out with full respect for human freedom, I don't pretend to understand. After all, God is a bit — to say the least — beyond me. I accept; no, more, I freely embrace what *is* because of his free choice.

No matter how you go about sharing and teaching, remember always, it is the Holy Spirit who is the teacher of prayer. Bearing that in mind, don't hesitate to use any opening that comes your way to share the prayer, gently, lovingly, with concern, as something very precious to you. Honest, open, simple sharing can never be offensive. "Faith comes through hearing." Your sharing can be a moment of special grace for someone for whom you care very much. It is worth laying down your life a bit. For "greater love than this no one has than that one lay down one's life for a friend."

If we are going to be what the Church wants us to be as contemplatives, we have to be willing to enter into contemplation — to die to ourselves, our own ideas, our own projects, our own doings, and open to God. The Second Vatican Council was a call to authenticity, to be what we are called. For it is not enough for us to be observant; it is not enough to say prayers and attend offices. We have to seek into the contemplative experience. We need to be constantly reminded of this and encouraged and strengthened to do it.

There is a hunger that is far more acute than the need for bread. There is a deep spiritual hunger. If this spiritual hunger is satisfied, then one can much more easily sustain the pains of physical hunger. But if it is not satisfied, even rich meals never satisfy. It is to this hunger we are called to respond with the nourishing gift of centering prayer.

One of the things Jesus says to us in centering prayer is "Bring them here." Bring me your senses, your mind, your heart. In centering, we bring everything to the Lord, all that we are, all that we have. We give them all to him, to let him do with them what he will. It is he who will heal them and make them whole, make them worthy instruments of the Holy Spirit, who will begin to act in them and through them by means of his gifts.

Social justice is a constitutive part of the Christian life, of living the gospels. Any kind of prayer or practice that leads us to fail in justice to others is not Christian; it is not of Christ and his Spirit. It is not pleasing to God.

True worship of God in spirit and truth will always move us not only to seek to be completely just in our dealing with others, but will also bear the fruits of love, kindness, long-suffering, goodness, and gentleness.

We are tempted to hold onto our usual way of doing things because we suspect that what the "prophet" is going to ask is not going to be all that easy. But what alternative do we have? Can we keep running all our lives? Keep ourselves ever distracted? Some certainly try, with alcohol, drugs, sex, TV, the internet. What a life! Is it a life? How different is a life that knows it has the Answer: the Way, the Truth and the Life, Eternal Life. We all have to ask ourselves: What am I going to seek? Endless activity? Amassed goods? Or am I going to moderate all this and find some desert spaces and desert places where I can listen to the wisdom of my own heart and encounter — yes, more than a prophet: Divine Truth himself abiding lovingly within my heart not just pointing but ready, gently and most lovingly, to lead me along the Way to the fullness of Life.

Centering prayer is prayer of the heart, prayer in the heart. It completely leaves off the lip service. True centering prayer always disposes us to give everyone their due, even while we cherish the time to give God his due. We know the time of centering is needed and nourishing, the source of all else. Yet we know that the call to constant prayer is lived out in many ways, that our prayer can, and does, take many forms.

Jesus tells us that it is the heart that matters. While we will pray in many different ways in the course of the day — communal prayer, liturgical prayer, shared scripture, personal *lectio*, perhaps a rosary or the stations, frequent ejaculations, cries for help, and words of thanks — we will want to make time for the prayer of the heart, prayer in the heart.

No one can practice centering prayer with any degree of fidelity and remain with their hearts far from God. As we faithfully let go of everything that comes along, everything from within and from without, to simply be to the Lord, all the dross and attachments wash away. I know of no other form of prayer that is so effective and so directly effective for helping us to arrive at purity of heart, so that instead of our hearts being far from the Lord, they are able to be wholly one with his wanting all that he wants.... Then we will live according to his commandments and not according to the customs and dictates of a hypocritical society.

The three disciples did respond to the Lord. They followed him in faith. Their commitment was very real. They persevered through the tough climb. Then "in their presence he was transfigured." If we persevere in our daily practice of centering prayer, we, too, will come to see the Lord in some wondrous new way, through the operation of the Holy Spirit in the gifts of knowledge, understanding, and wisdom.

What we can do now to bring about his kingdom of justice is to cooperate in the establishment of justice in that portion of his kingdom over which we have some immediate control: ourselves. Let us begin the pursuit of justice and peace by cleaning up our own lives and establishing peace within our hearts.

Through centering prayer not only do we come to know Jesus in the fullness of his divinity, but we also come to know Jesus in the fullness of his humanity, in his oneness with every other human person. Through the activity of the Holy Spirit in his gifts, we begin to see Jesus in everyone and everyone in Jesus. It would be hard to overstate the love and joy that this brings into our lives. And how it affects all our human relations, all our ministerial outreach, all our presence to others.

We do not like to be dependent. Let's be honest. How much of our prayer really comes out of a realization of total dependence? How often do we go through the motions of prayer because it is the right and proper thing to do, even while we feel we have everything under control? As we stood in our pews at Mass last Sunday did we have any sense that at that very moment our continued existence, our very existence in that moment depended on God's benignity, on his continued mercy and goodness?

For me dependency can be a school of humility, a basic human virtue, a doorway to reality. As I experience a new and growing dependence I am invited to realize more my total dependence on God and others as the agents of God.

Can I be a gift of God to others in my need? Is that why he lets me linger on with this increasing dependency? Do they have a need for me to be here to give them a chance to learn more about self-giving love? As long as I am able, cannot my smiles, my affirmation, my expressed gratitude help them to get a little more in touch with their innate goodness?

We need to stop, to let go of all the surface stuff, and go into the desert of our heart. And listen. Then knowing our emptiness and deepest longings, we must seek the prophetic wisdom that can point the way. If we do not take time to listen to our deepest longings, if we constantly drown them out with our activities and distractions, we can never hope to find true happiness.

My fingers now go racing across the keys of the computer. How tragic if suddenly just one of these two hands fell limp, no longer able to strike the keys or perform the many, many tasks it does for me each day, each hour. Yet how often have I stopped to thank the Lord for the marvel of this hand, the way it does operate, the way my mind and my eye can direct it, the way it can be trained so that it leaps from one key to another with a certain sureness and speed. I thank you Lord for my hand, my head, my heart, my whole being. When we go further and allow ourselves to get in touch with the gift God has given us in the life and death of Jesus, how could we ever doubt the benignity, the good will of our God toward us?

Mary not only lost a Son; she lost her God who had entrusted himself to her as a Son. When she found him, as fit as ever and so at peace, all the pent-up emotion of the days of anguished searching broke forth: "Why did you do this to us?" As much as we feel for the mother, how good it is for us to hear this sinless one vent her frustration and anger, her incomprehension. It is all right at appropriate times to be very angry with God. And to vent that anger in a prayer that shakes its fist and asks indignantly: Why? Or to give voice to a deep pain, to true anguish: Why? why? why? Or to the utter mystery of it all, the incomprehension: Why?

Like Mary, we want it to be for us a question full of faith, and not like the question of her elderly cousin who questioned because he doubted. We ask with confidence, knowing that the loving will of God can and will be accomplished in us and in our lives, seeking only to know the way insofar as we need to live into a complete yes, as Mary so well exemplifies for us.

Do you not know that I must be in my Father's house? Yes, Lord, I know. And if I cannot always rejoice in that presence, I can rest in it and find refreshment for my soul. And often enough for my body, also.

The important thing is
that we do pray regularly
and allow God to be
to us the source of love,
life, peace, and happiness
that he wants to be and
that we so much want.

We need those
times of prayer when
we listen not just with
our ears, our eyes,
our minds, but more
with our hearts,
with our whole being.

It is outside the time
of prayer that we will
begin to see the
difference, as the fruits
of the Spirit
begin to flourish
in our lives.

As the truth takes hold in us, its roots pulverize the prejudices. And we are happy to see them go. The perception of our true self, that beautiful image of God now perceived in the eyes of God, frees us from the false identity that has such a pernicious hold on us. We don't have to do or to have now. We are. And we are magnificent. We are the beloved of God. The clutching thorns are gone.

Contemplative insight does not only reveal to us the absorbing beauty of God and our own intrinsic beauty in him. It also reveals to us the beauty of every other person, each of whom is one with us in God.

In a word, the fruits of the Holy Spirit will be very present in our lives when we live out of our contemplative experience. This is surely the way we can judge the authenticity of our experience. Our contemplation should overflow into the whole of our lives, creatively bringing a certain sacredness to our environment because our eyes have been opened to the sacred that is already there, and we live and act accordingly.

Contemplation is the summit of all human actions because it is the most total relationship with God. It is exalted above all other human activities. It is the thing that ultimately motivates, grounds, and gives meaning to all else that we do as Christians.

Did you ever notice in the gospels how those two great women of prayer, Mary the Mother of Jesus and Mary of Bethany, obtained from the Lord his first and his greatest miracles without asking? They simply let the concern of their hearts be there before Jesus — "They have no wine," "He who you love is sick" — knowing that he would take care of everything, which he did.

It is by doing the will of the Father that we are Christ's mother, that we mother the Christ in ourselves and in one another. Whether it is by sitting at the feet of Jesus as that other Mary or by bustling about like her sister — by doing what God wants of us we make our contribution to the central undertaking of the creation: the forming of the whole Christ.

Our Christian spirituality begins when we let ourselves be formed by sacred scripture and let that "mind" be in us which was in Christ Jesus (Phil 2:5). For this to become a reality, a daily encounter with the Lord in the scriptures becomes essential.

We should always treat our Bible with great reverence. It should not be simply put on the shelf with other books or tossed on the desk. It should be enthroned in our home, in our room, in our office. In many churches today the sacred text is given a special place, sometimes with a lamp burning before it, proclaiming a real Presence — for God is really present in his word, waiting to speak to his people.

Certainly, it is not enough to know God conceptually. Even as we begin to know him in this way, we cannot but be attracted to him. Affections will come forth, and they will lead us to seek an ever fuller union of knowledge in and through love. And insatiable desire will begin to grow in us. If we wish to respond to it, the way leads to experiential or contemplative prayer, to going beyond our thoughts and feelings to the deeper level of our being.

It is important for us not to judge the quality of our prayer by the presence or absence of thoughts or the use of the word, or indeed anything else. There is no place for judgment here. We are simply spending some time with our Beloved. What happens, happens. The important thing is that we are making time for him, giving ourselves to him. We are not there to get anything for ourselves, especially not some sort of self-satisfaction or feelings or peace or the like. This is a very pure and Christian prayer. It is a real dying to self to give ourselves in love to God.

Reality is that we are risen with Christ. Staying too much on the surface, we are all too often conscious only of the passing experiences of the disintegration of sin in our lives. It is when we stop and go to our deeper selves that we find ourselves one with Christ, the object of the infinitely caring and tender love of the Father. This is the true Christian perception.

It is only when we are willing to let go of our rational control of consciousness and open the space for the Spirit to act in us through the gifts that we can begin to know and sense things as God knows and experiences them. This freedom to let go of our rational control and open to the divine activity is developed in us through the practice of contemplative prayer.

It would be a great mistake to try to do the prayer "right." It is, rather, making space in our lives, both in regard to time and to mental attitude and desire, to allow God to reveal to us our true selves in the eyes of his love and to bring us to the freedom of the sons and daughters of God. Some things can only be known by experience. That is true of this kind of experiential prayer. "Be still and know that I am God" (Ps 46:10). "Taste and see how sweet the Lord is" (Ps 33:9).

Most of us most of the time are all caught up in activities. We are caught up with our possessions, trying to keep up with the Joneses. But no matter how busy we are, there come those moments when something deep within us tells us: this is not enough; this can't be all that there is in life. At times we all need to let go. Like John we need to ask: Where do you dwell? And go to that place deep within. There we will find our truest self and hear more clearly the yearning of our own heart. That is the desert for most, the desert of their own heart, where the great Prophet dwells, Truth himself.

He has said: ask and you shall receive; seek and you will find. Unfortunately we ask for the ephemeral, which isn't really satisfying. We seek what is passing and will leave us empty. Once we realize in truth that we do not know what we truly want, where our true happiness lies, then we can begin to seek a teacher, a prophet — the guidance of one whom the Lord has sent, the Church who makes Jesus present to us today, Jesus who is all that our hearts seek. Until then we will in fact be in a desert chasing mirages, encountering delusions, finding all swaying and unstable.

We hear that prayer is useless or perhaps unnecessary, at least prayer of petition. After all, didn't Jesus say that the Father already knows what we need before we ask him? … God did not simply make this world and toss it out there to leave it go along on its own. Indeed, at every moment the Lord brings his creation forth in creative love. And he has willed that the way he is going to bring forth this world in the next hour, the next day, the next year, the next millennium, depends in part on what we ask of him. Our prayers of petition are very powerful in the providence of God.

67

All prayer is answered. But it is not always answered in the way we expect. God looks to the heart more than to the lips.... The Lord knows we seek happiness for ourselves and for our loved ones. But he knows, he who sees in terms of eternal life, that what we specifically ask for is not always the way to happiness.

Not only do I take so much for granted; I act as if I were the source. I will be a person of gratitude. From the moment I wake up in the morning, my word will be "thank you": Thank you, Lord, for a good night's sleep. Thank you, Lord, for a new day. Thank you, Lord, for a warm and comfortable bed. Thank you, Lord, for the roof over my head. Thank you, Lord, for your presence here with me. Thank you, Lord, for the strength and ability to get up out of this bed, to exercise my muscles, to walk. Thank you, Lord, for this shower, this hot water, this soap, these towels, this wonderful body of mine that you give into my care and use. Thank you, Lord…. Can we ever stop? And I know from my own experience: when we are in the thank-you mode we enjoy each thing so much more and so much more consciously.

This solidarity [of the two blind men, Mt 9:27–31] pleased the heart of Jesus. He would say: Where two are gathered in my name, there I am. And these two cried out together his messianic name, so powerfully meaningful for these Jews: Son of David. And their prayer was not each for himself alone. They were praying for each other. Jesus says: Whenever two agree on anything, it will be done for them. The love, care and support these two had for each other could not be denied. Their eyes were opened! They saw. Were they surprised? No — not with their faith, not with Jesus' gentle touch. Just delighted.

The way to a deep inner peace is to be in touch with the inner reality. Too often our prayer is one of words, thoughts, images, concepts — all things produced by our minds. No wonder we often find prayer tiresome, hardly refreshing. Yet Jesus said: "Come to me all you who work hard and are weighed down with the cares of life and I will refresh you." Prayer should be refreshing. We need to learn to listen with love, to listen in love.

I do not think we can really come to true adoration until we have come to the center, to the true self, and left behind all the limitations of the false self. As long as we approach God through our own limited concepts, symbols, or images, we are far too shielded from his awesomeness.

The last time I had breakfast with Mother Teresa in Calcutta, as I was leaving I asked her for a "word of life" to bring to my brothers at the monastery. Mother looked at me intently, with those deep, deep brown eyes that seem to invite you into pools of embracing love. With deliberateness she spoke her words: "Father, tell them ... to pray ... that I *don't get in God's way.*"

For most of us, our mission will be largely one of presence. To a great extent, our evangelization will be unspoken. Like the prayer itself, it will be one of being. But there is a time and place for the spoken word. A simple "God bless you" or "God is with you" to a telephone operator or at the checkout counter or toll booth can be a moment of extraordinary grace and presence.

There is great comfort to be found in centering prayer. We mourn our sins, perhaps more than most, when we center, for we see them so clearly in the light of the divine presence. We see their heinousness in the light of such an immensity of goodness and mercy. Yet, at the very same moment, we know the totality of the forgiveness that is ours. We are comforted.

The call of the Christian to be a peacemaker is clear and unequivocal. We are called to follow Christ, to be his disciples. And he is the Prince of Peace. He is the Son of God and it is the peacemakers who will be called the sons of God. The danger is that we Christians in our peacemaking efforts will be drawn to interact at a secular or materialistic level, working only at economics and politics, and not make the unique contribution we can as persons of faith, empowered in oneness with Christ, creating the context for true and lasting peace.

The only way to true holiness, Christian holiness, is to die to the false self — the self that is made up of what we do and what we have and what we think others think of us — so that the true self, that beautiful image of God that ever comes forth from his creative love, and not from our efforts, can emerge.

When we struggle with others, we at least acknowledge that they are worth struggling with. But when we totally ignore them, they virtually cease to exist as far as we are concerned. In centering prayer there is no struggle. We simply turn to God, thus ignoring the false self. And each time it does succeed in catching our attention, we simply, gently return to the Lord, using our prayer word, turning our back on the false self in turning to him.

The false self very much likes to make a project out of things, make them hard, and make sure we are doing them right so that it can then pat itself on the back for doing such a good job. There is no place for this in centering prayer. Like little children, we simply jump into our Father's arms and let him do the rest. There is no cause to pat ourselves on the back. Who can pat himself on the back for resting in the arms of the one he loves?

Our most private room is that deep place within us, what we have been calling our "center." There, indeed, our Father dwells. And we are invited to go to that center, shut out all else and abide there with our Father in prayer. This is precisely what we do in centering prayer. With the use of our prayer word we, as it were, close the door, or to use another image, we create a cloud of unknowing, leaving everything outside and ourselves quietly and peacefully within with the Father.

The fact is, the moments when we are in prayer, we are in a realm of consciousness that is beyond that which the human memory can record. It is beyond reason. As Paul put it, "Eye has not seen, ear has not heard, nor has it even entered into the human mind, what God has prepared for those who love him."

"The kingdom of heaven is within." And indeed, that is what we seek in centering prayer.

We certainly do not seek our own center or seek ourselves in any way. That is one of the reasons why centering prayer is totally different from self-hypnosis (in spite of what some who really do not understand the prayer say). We do not seek ourselves in any way. Nor do we seek anything for ourselves — peace or consolation or light.

We quite simply seek to enter into the kingdom of heaven, where God is all. We seek to enter into that state where we can say in truth, "My God and my all."

Happiness consists in knowing what you want and knowing you have it or are on the way to getting it. Those who truly seek God, who want God, and have the insight of faith and the gifts to perceive his real presence in every one and every thing, always have what they want. They know that the whole world is the place of God, that all is sacred. They are always happy. Their lives express that joy which is a fruit of the Holy Spirit.

We are brought within and rest in the very embrace of God. Centering prayer allows us in some way to experience this, as it opens us to the action of the Holy Spirit in us through the gifts of wisdom, understanding, and knowledge. Resting in this embrace we find wonderful peace, deep joy, a peace this world cannot give, Christ's own peace.

There are those who stay outside when they want to communicate with the Lord, to pray to him. They pray with words, thoughts and ideas, rather than with their very being. They send these words to God, whom they sense as being at some distance, perhaps off in his heavens or in the tabernacle. Perhaps even within them, but not as one with them. They are sending word in. It is still subject to subject, not realizing their deep intersubjective union with God. Their thoughts, ideas, concepts and images stand as a crowd around the Lord. They stand between the Lord and those who pray.

The follower of Christ, the Christian who wants to follow Christ, to live the Christian life to the full, not so much extensively in activities as intensively in act, remembers how often his Master went apart to pray. His years of growth were so hidden, we know virtually nothing of them. After he received his commission to ministry through a voice from heaven: "Listen to him," he disappears into the desert for weeks of solitude and silence, and, we may be sure, prayer. As his busy years of healing ministry unfolded, again and again, alone or with his chosen ones, he went apart.

We can all ask ourselves as we look around at the clutter of our own lives, great or little as it might be, and look at our habitudes: Do I possess or am I possessed? Do I use or am I used? Is this what Paul was talking about when he said we should use this creation as if we used it not? To be able to use the good things of our Father's beneficence and enjoy them in such a way that we retain our ability to use them not, to get along without them — this is true freedom.

The primary Christian community is the home. Here the basic attitude of wanting the other to increase, to grow greater, must be expressed in making time for each other.

Commenting on, "The kingdom of heaven is like yeast a woman took and mixed in with three measures of flower ..." (Mt 13:33).

We could consider the three measures the three states of consciousness: waking, sleeping, and dreaming. Centering prayer brings us into a fourth state of consciousness. We might call it transcendental consciousness or God consciousness. Once it has begun to develop in our lives, it can coexist with any one of the other three states and enliven them. It is that level of consciousness on which the Holy Spirit works in us through his gifts.

All the levels of our consciousness are enriched and enlivened by the state of consciousness we come to when we willingly lay aside our human reasoning and open ourselves to the activity of the Holy Spirit through his gifts. We might also see the three measures as three faculties in the human person: the intellect, the will, and the emotions. Centering prayer has a profound effect on the activity of each of these three.

Meditation releases stress. As we sit quietly in centering prayer, resting in the depths with the Lord, our mind continues to operate. Thoughts and images flow along. If they are allowed to flow freely, the stress that surrounds them flows away with them. (…) Our creative energies seem to function more freely. Others note a softening of our features. We look younger. There is a sparkle in our eyes. All in all, life seems very good. At the root of this is the leavening of the spirit. We come to know who we are, how loved we are, who this God of love is. Life flows up powerfully and freely from within, from the very Source of life who is ever present at the center of our being, with all his creative love.

The important thing ... is to bring to Jesus, with the greatest possible fidelity, your five senses, your mind, and your heart, all your feelings, your thoughts, and your desires, your whole being, in your regular practice of centering prayer so that he can redirect them, bless them, and break them open. Then what joy you will have as the divine grace and power flow through you, and thousands of men, women, and children are fed, and your own inner resources grow and grow.

Jesus' way of going about things certainly is strange. He came on earth to establish the universal Church, the largest and most powerful and enduring institution in the history of the human race. And what does he do? He spends the first thirty, or more probably thirty-three, years of his life in a quite ordinary way, learning how to live an ordinary prayerful life. When finally he sets forth on his great task, he spends the first forty days in complete retirement, doing nothing but praying. Then he comes forth. He has a power of speech that is unprecedented. And he can work miracles at will. He attracts mobs. Yet, time after time, night after night, he slips away, leaving the clamoring crowds, to spend his time in prayer.

Sometimes people have had difficulty with the idea of centering prayer because they feared it was leaving Jesus behind. They quote Saint Teresa of Jesus to the effect that she always began her prayer by approaching Jesus in his agonizing humanity. That was her way, and it really worked for her. But each should be free to follow the way the Lord leads him or her. If we are truly being to the Lord, we will never leave Jesus behind. He enjoys the Father's favor. The Father will always point us toward his Beloved: "Listen to him" with your whole being. Be totally open to him. Let him truly live in and through you. Be one with him.

The one who practices centering prayer does not wait around for others to come along and persecute them so that they can attain the kingdom of heaven. They set about persecuting themselves — their false selves — so that they can be free of the tyranny of their own thoughts and feelings, of their own interpretations of reality, of the defensiveness and competitiveness that closes them in on themselves. Freed from all of this they can be open to reality, to the wonderfully affirming presence of God within them, their sure defense — to the kingdom of God within as their kingdom.

And, of course, living in this way, we can be sure that we will possess the kingdom of God as our own kingdom *forever*.

Centering prayer is meant to lead all the way to the summit of the Taboric experience. And it will infallibly lead there if one is faithful in following Jesus, even though we don't know where he is leading us, until he does deign to be transfigured in our presence. If we remain faithfully in our prayer, whether it be experience of Christ and the scriptures, or a cloud of unknowing that overshadows us, we will come to hear the Father say to us of us, "This is my child, my beloved; the one who enjoys my favor."

When we ourselves have been enlightened, having opened the space by regular time spent in contemplative prayer for the Spirit to enlighten us through his gifts, then we can be present to others as a light who will enlighten their darkness simply by our presence, sometimes by our word, and always by our love.

May you find great peace
and joy at the Center.
Let us hold each other
in caring prayer.

Prayer can also be effective through the transformation of consciousness it effects in us ... (we cannot constantly pray for peace and meditate on peace and not become more profoundly men and women of peace) and through us the rest of our species.

Sources and Permissions

(Excerpts are used by permission of the publishers. The numbers refer to the selection number in the present book, followed by the page number in the cited Pennington work.)

Call to the Center (Hyde Park, NY: New City Press, 1995/2003)1:78, 2:66, 4:79, 5:81, 6:66, 8:76, 9:49, 11:77, 13:81–82, 14:82, 15:92, 18:102, 20:110, 21:111, 23:116, 26:129, 28:139, 30:141, 31:142, 32:152, 33:152, 35:153, 36:154, 37:154, 38:161, 40:164, 52:110, 56:57, 71:11, 72:23, 73:37, 74:38, 75:43, 77:47, 78:47–48, 79:48, 80:56–57, 81:70, 82:74, 84:93–94, 85:101–102, 89:126, 90:127, 91:128–129, 92:144, 93:146, 94:163, 95:45, 96:164, 97:39

A Place Apart (Garden City, NY: Doubleday & Company, Inc., 1983) 7:62, 17:159, 24:42, 39:17, 76:152, 83:128, 86:26–27, 87:70, 88:124, 99:156

A Retreat with Thomas Merton (Rockport, MA: Element, 1988) 3:114, 19:24–25, 22:57, 25:89–90, 27:64, 29:91, 55:93

Thomas Merton, My Brother (Hyde Park, NY: New City Press, 1996) 53:128, 54:128, 58:136, 59:136–137, 60:138, 61:142, 62:145, 63:198, 64:143

Who Do You Say I Am? (Hyde Park, NY: New City Press, 2005) 10:88–89, 12:96–97, 16:43, 34:35, 41:62, 42:118, 43:118, 44:34–35, 45:75, 46:125–126, 47:122, 48:129, 49:158, 50:155, 51:157, 57:131, 65:34, 66:34, 67:38, 68:44–45, 69:76, 70:80–81, 98:158

Also available in the same series:

Coming Together in Joy
99 Sayings by Benedict XVI
hardcover: 978-1-56548-273-9

Overlook Much Correct a Little
99 Sayings by John XXIII
hardcover: 978-1-56548-261-6
paperback: 978-1-56548-255-5

On Our Pilgrimage to Eternity
99 Sayings by John Paul II
hardcover: 978-1-56548-198-5
paperback: 978-1-56548-230-2

Words of Hope and Healing
99 Sayings by Henri Nouwen
hardcover: 978-1-56548-227-2

Like a Drop in the Ocean
99 Sayings by Mother Teresa
hardcover: 978-1-56548-238-8
paperback: 978-1-56548-242-5

The Path of Merciful Love
99 Sayings by Thérèse of Lisieux
hardcover: 978-1-56548-245-6
paperback: 978-1-56548-246-3

* * *

Wings for the Soul
99 Sayings on Happiness
hardcover: 978-1-56548-283-8
paperback: 978-1-56548-271-5

We Have Seen a Great Light
99 Sayings on Christmas
hardcover: 978-1-56548-270-8
paperback: 978-1-56548-271-5

The Golden Thread of Life
99 Sayings on Love
hardcover: 978-1-56548-182-4

Blessed Are the Peacemakers
99 Sayings on Peace
hardcover: 978-1-56548-183-1

Sunshine On Our Way
99 Sayings on Friendship
hardcover: 978-1-56548-195-4

Organizations and Corporations

This title is available at special quantity discounts for bulk purchases for sales promotions, premiums, or fundraising.

For information call or write:

New City Press, Marketing Dept.
202 Cardinal Rd.
Hyde Park, NY 12538.
Tel: 1-800-462-5980;
1-845-229-0335
Fax: 1-845-229-0351
info@newcitypress.com